God's Got My Number:

And One Day He Called Me

God's Got My Number: And One Day He Called Me

ROBERT K. LOMAS

StoryTerrace

CONTENTS

PREFACE

I spent decades in prisons and in the streets, red light districts, and drug dens and shot it out with the most legendary criminal figures in Toledo, Ohio. I was often surrounded by death and yet here I am, praise God! What many would learn is that my favor only goes where I go, and when I depart, so does God's favor that follows my life like a cloud of protection. I believe nobody is too far gone for God's grace to reach them. I also believe it is impossible to truly have an encounter with God, as I did, and ever be the same. I am not good at what I do because of my abilities but by making myself a willing vessel to be used by God. As a result, supernatural things happen to me and through me. I seek not my will but only God's will for my life. People often say, "We've never met someone like Rob Lomas. What kind of preacher are you?" I often reply, "The kind God made for hardened people like you." My goal is to help people discover their true self: Mentally, spiritually, emotionally, and physically. I believe that many people go through life never truly having a clue who they are. They become like actors and actresses in a long-running Broadway stage show, constantly playing a role. In my profession, I get a million excuses why people can't let go of their facades and bad habits. I want to offer words of encouragement. I want people to see it's not how you start in life, it's how you finish. A lot of people are looking for an excuse to quit. We can all come up with excuses. Anybody who has traveled and survived the path I traveled; you don't have to do any of that. If I could do what I did, come out the other side, and be working on my doctorate today, anybody can do it. Have faith in God and yourself. Anything is possible.

Remove This Mugshot

Information Run Full Background Check Now!

Name	Robert Keith Lomas
Location	Toledo, Ohio
Age	41 years
Booking Date	05-22-2005

Charges

2925.11A, POSSESSION OF DRUGS OBTAIN POSSESS OR USE A CONTROLLED SUBSTANCE

An arrest does not mean that the individual has been convicted of the crime. Individuals on this website are innocent until proven guilty by a court of law. The information related to charges and arrest or booking information is provided through public domain and in accordance with the Freedom of Information Act.

Other Mugshots near Toledo

http://www.mugshotsonline.com/ohio/toledo/robert-keith-lomas/26212531   4/5/2012

One of my many trips to the Lucas County Jail: 1624 Spielbusch, Toledo, Ohio, 43624

The tools of a hustler's trade.

1

FATHER KNOWS BEST

My dad, Edmond Lomas, Jr., was extremely strict on us growing up. He wanted us to understand that life is not always fair, and he wanted us to be without any excuses for not making it in life. He would constantly say to my brothers and me, "Weak men strive on sympathy. I am raising men, not boys, and you can do nothing without God." Even though he would say that, and often, I wouldn't pay much attention. Until he died, my dad overcompensated for me after my mom passed. When I look back on it, he was trying to save me from myself. Coincidentally, that was one of the things Judge Charles J. Doneghy said to me in 1998, the first time he sent me away. Judge Doneghy was Black, and he had worked himself up in city of Toledo. He looked like George Jefferson with gold teeth. Like other judges that had sentenced me to prison, like Robert Franklin and Robert Penn, Judge Doneghy had come from one of the roughest neighborhoods in Toledo. None of them used their backgrounds as an excuse. They pulled themselves up by their bootstraps and used their wits to get out of the city circumstances. They took pride in telling serial defendants like me that when we appeared before them in court. In 1998, Judge Doneghy listened to me try to talk myself out of trouble in court, and he was impressed with the motions I filed and my different challenges to the search warrant. Judge Doneghy finally asked me, "Who taught you all this?" I told him I went to the law library and looked it up. Judge Doneghy looked at me and said, "It baffles me how you could teach yourself how to defend yourself and you're just about right. So why is it that you can't teach yourself something else?" He meant something other than the criminal activities I was doing. Judge Doneghy then got to the point, the one my dad had been trying to make all those years: "Not only do I have to save the community from you, but I have to protect you from yourself. Because you think you're doing nothing wrong. you think what's a little crime amongst each other? I have to protect you from your imagination."

Honestly, I have lost count of the number of institutions I had served time in. For my stretch that started in 1998, because I had such an extensive record, I was one of two drug dealers who was sent to a maximum-security prison. I was told, "You should be a hardened criminal because they had been dealing with you so long." Everybody else there was there for heinous crimes, and me and another kid from Lima were walking around with seven-year out dates—

everybody else were lifers.

I was sent away in 1998 and got out in May of 2004. I would like to say that I stopped my criminal ways, but the addiction to the lifestyle was something I couldn't shake. Who would I be and what would I be without my power, the drugs, and the money? Everybody in town knew my name. The Red Sea would part when us drug dealers came by. We were like celebrities in our community. We were, ironically, like role models, and people assumed we had all the wisdom because we appeared to be winning and were on top of the food chain in the city.

By 2005, I got back on top and got my cash flow back to where I was used to. Then, I started to think a little bit. It had been 25 years since I had been on this cycle. Drugs, jail, money, all the women I wanted. I had the Solomon-type revelation—it was all vanity. What did it matter, all the money that I stole and hid? I thought more and more about what my dad said to me when he found out what I really did for a living. I came over to visit him one day, and I had my 300 D Mercedes with the wood grain finish. My dad asked me to please leave his home. I said, "What are you talking about?" My dad saw all the younger people, like my cousins, were looking up to me. Then, referring to my car purchased with drug money, he said, "Take that poison away from my house. I think you're less than a man." I still didn't get it and asked, again, "What do you mean?" Now my dad really didn't hold back. He told me, "If the only thing I can do is survive off of other people's sickness. I'd rather be a homeless person. You're worse than a parasite. Please get out of my sight." I was angry about what I was hearing, but on the other hand, it kind of freed me because I didn't want to have to pretend around my dad anymore. The cat was out of the bag. Still, it got me thinking again. When my dad took us kids up to Door Street in the Black downtown in Toledo (back then in the 1960s and 1970s everything was segregated), we would see the pimps' cars and the drug dealers. Dad would tell us that the lowest thing you could ever be was a pimp or a pusher. He reminded us we were Black, so how could any Black man be involved in human trafficking when you're a descendant of slavery? How horrible was it for a Black man to think that it's OK to oppress another human being? I didn't understand why my dad would say that at the time. It took me too long to realize that he was a constant teacher. He would say, "I trusted God and lived right and came from Louisiana with a sixth-grade education, and God has placed me above men of great stature and great education in their lives. God has elevated me for living a clean, righteous life. There is no substitute for that." But I didn't hear my father. In 2007, I bought a gas station. Truth be told, I didn't really purchase it. It was the result of a drug debt where the guy owed me so much money, he finally said, "I can't come up with the money. I'm getting out of this business, so the place is yours." It was a frustrating way to settle the debt, but now that the gas station was mine, I did what I could to make it the best. That's how I am with everything. I put a lot of money into that place. My dad was proud of me, seeing that I was making a go at a legitimate business, and it looked like an effort in the right direction. What he didn't know was that it was really a place to launder money through. I never put gas in the pumps, but we did do repair work on cars. I wanted a way out from my drug business, but I felt trapped and obligated to my associates. One day, me and my future wife, Selena, were over at the shop. My dad came by, met her and gave his approval. Then he leaned on his cane, and he said to me, "I need to see you every day because I'll be dying soon." It blew me away because he said it so straightforward and because he had beat lung cancer years before. He told me, "I have terminal cancer now. They're giving me six months to live, and I would like to see you every day. The other kids have always been with me; you haven't. There are things I need to say to you."

Every day after that, I would spend time with my dad after I closed the shop. One particular day, he was really in pain. He was living at his house where we had nursing staff and a hospital bed for him. That day, he was on the side of the bed crying. It was the second time in my life I had seen him cry, but this time, he was hysterical. I said, "Dad, are you OK?" He said, "I'm all right." I told him I knew the cancer was pretty painful. He said he wasn't bothered by that. He said, "I'm crying out to God. I'm asking who will take care of my family when I die?" It blew me away.

Here is this man passing, and he wasn't afraid of dying. He believed in God and the afterlife. He was concerned about who would take care of his family and steer them in the right way. I said to my father, "Dad, I got those bums. Who do you think has been taking care of them all this time?" Sure, I might have been the family scapegoat, but members of our family had been paying the mortgage with the dirty money. Now my dad started laughing hard because he knew that. I promised my dad I would keep taking care of the family. He looked at me and said, " One son that I have that's qualified to lead this family is too selfish and too big of a coward to do it." Then he said, "You've been leading them, but where have you been leading them to?" I had nephews follow me into the drug trade, hustling, and all kinds of other crazy stuff. They saw me and thought it looked like I was winning. Just as easy as I had been teaching them negativity, I could have been teaching them positivity. Soon enough, my dad asked to go to hospice. The reason he did that was because he didn't want to die in the house. He believed my stepmom couldn't stay in the house if he passed there. As soon as my dad got to hospice, he went   into a coma-type state for three days and didn't speak to anybody. During the third day, I was testing out a new car I had just bought, a V-12 Jaguar. It started running funny while I was near my dad's hospice, so I thought it was a sign. I stopped at hospice to see how my father was doing. When I went in there, I touched his face, and he had sleep in his eye. He was still breathing. I asked the nurse if she could get me a warm washcloth. I wiped his head and touched his face. I started talking to him and said, "Dad, you know, I want to apologize for being such an embarrassment and never even trying to live like you tried to teach me. I want you to know all the things you taught me, I never forgot. I do believe in God, and I do know what it's like to be a decent person. If you can hear me, I want you to know I love you." He woke right up. It startled me, but I was glad he was conscious. He said, "I can hear you." I said, "I thought you couldn't talk." He shot back, "I'll talk to whoever the hell I want to talk to. Get me out of this bed, boy." I sat him in the chair next to the bed, and we talked all morning. Finally, he said, "You got it now. God done changed you." I thought the poor man was delusional because I was still selling all sorts of dope and cocaine. He said, "God ain't gonna have to worry about you because when He blesses you with large sums of money, you're not going to steal from God because you have had that. You're gonna do the right thing." I'm thinking to myself, If I ever stop selling dope I ain't ever gonna have another nickel again anyway. I kept all those thoughts to myself. My dad asked me to not put him back in the bed. I said, "Dad, you gotta get some rest." He looked at me and demanded, "What do I need rest for? I'm dying!" I was the last person my dad ever spoke to.

My dad passed on April 25th, 2008. The number 25 in the Bible symbolizes "grace upon grace," which struck me as significant for my dad's life. He was a high ranking 33rd degree Mason, so he had the rites of passage the Masonic Temple had. He was proud of being a Mason and a deacon in the church. I had no idea how big of an impact he had from his days of a fallen-down drunk to his conversion. It blew my mind how many people attended his funeral, all those people who came from all over, different Shriners, different Masonic lodges, people he had fellowship with. He had mentored countless pastors that would not have had a spiritual mentor otherwise. Sadly, my dad, who had tried to mentor me, left this earth before he could witness my conversion.

After my dad passed, I had a vision, even though I did not know what to make of it back then. I never had any visions of my mom. I looked at her photo a lot. She was very whimsical and always clever and quick-witted. But it was my dad who paid me a visit. Now I know how to read these visions. Everything that I do today, God gave me the instructions on how to do it. I could make sense of these visions once I was restored to sanity, but more on that later. So shortly after my dad passed, I had a dream that took place in the same giant church he was buried in. I was going to the funeral, but when I stepped into the church for the funeral the road was made up of round stones like in The Wizard of Oz, and the stones were emerald and rubies with names on them. When I got into the funeral, my dad was dressed in Masonic clothing and two men stood guard with swords over him. When I went in, I saw that he was in the casket. But then I saw an image of him sitting in the front pew. He gestured me over to have a seat next to him and be quiet. Then he leaned over to me, and he said clear as day, "You know I'm not in there. This is just for them, and I'm OK." He kind of smiled about it, then said, "Ain't that funny?" And then he disappeared. Kind of strange.

Me at age 15, with my father selling jewelry.

2

INNOCENT AS CHARGED

O f the 26 felonies I've been charged with over the years, I was guilty as charged. There was only one time in my life I didn't do something that I got sent to prison for. That was my 27th felony. One day in July of 2007, I closed the shop up for the day, then went to visit my dad. After visiting with him, I left. I was driving down the street. Police lights lit up behind me, and I got pulled over. I knew most of the cops around town, but I had never seen those two officers before. As soon as they approached my car I told them, "You can search my car if you want to. It's registered to me. You're not going to find any drugs in a car that's registered to me. If you know who I am, you know I'm not that stupid." Those officers told me to get out of the car and stay put. Then they searched my car. I just stood in the hot summer sun waiting for this thing to be over with. Finally, they walked back over to me. One cop reached in his pocket, and he said, "Look what I found." I stared at the cocaine he had in his hand, and I said, "That ain't mine." He said, "It is now." I was hip to what these cops were up to. They planted drugs on me because they wanted us old timers to play ball with them so they could catch the young guys. Me being old school, I hold to the code, so if they thought I was ever going to be a rat, that wasn't going to happen.

Those cops took me downtown and charged me with possession of cocaine. I told myself there was no way they were going to get this off, no judge will believe it. It was the lowest felony (almost close to a misdemeanor) I had ever been charged with, so I never took it too seriously. The case landed in front of my old "friend" Judge Charles J. Doneghy, who was close to retirement. Even though he had battled with me, I thought I was going to get a fair shake from Judge Doneghy. I ended up fighting that case for two years. After my dad died in 2008, the deal was floated to me to cop to a fifth-degree felony, which carried a nine-month sentence. I was told since I was not on papers and I made five years parole, I would probably just get probation. That's what I thought might happen.

When I stood in front of Judge Doneghy, he looked at me and said, "My main man Mr. Lomas. We go back a long way, don't we? I'm almost retired, and you're going to roll me off the bench." He then rattled off some of my resume: "You were one of the last prisoners in the Toledo House of Corrections, you were one of the last to leave Ohio State Reformatory Mansfield, you were one of the last people to leave Lima Correctional for the criminally insane. You closed down three legendary prisons, and I'm retiring." Judge Doneghy was quiet for a moment. The suspense was killing me. He finally said, "I think you got it. But I'm going to send you back one more time because I want you to remember. I'm going to give you nine months." I was still thinking I was going to get probation, so I said, "Nine months? Nine months where?" Judge Doneghy said, "Nine months in prison." I couldn't believe it. He went on to explain, "I want you to remember what it's like one more time, and I believe that will save your life." I still couldn't believe it.

So I went back to prison at Allen Oakwood Correctional in Lima, Ohio, and, no doubt, those nine months were harder than any of those other years I did. One reason it was so tough was because some of my nephews and other kids from the neighborhood were in there with me. They were still looking up to me, even though we were in prison. I thought about what my dad had told me before he passed, that I could have been a role model for something positive. These kids looked at me, followed my path, and now they were in prison at age 19 or 20. It was like cancer, but worse than cancer. It was contagious. The criminal mindset is contagious. I served time with a guy named Ron Tijerina, who served 16 years for being wrongfully convicted. Ron said everyone we come in contact with we either infect or affect, whether it's negative or positive. Every encounter should be something of value. What we said yesterday was the things we said. We can always take back the things we said, but we can't take back the things we did. I was horrified with the power of that concept. I was watching these kids in prison who were there because of my influence in some way. My girlfriend, Selena, was a unique woman. I don't know what she saw in me, but she wouldn't give up on me, and she kept coming to visit me in prison. I played guitar and ended up playing in the praise group and other groups in the prison church. It put me around positive people. I started to realize I hated the old life I had lived. I realized I hated me. My self-destructive behavior was a result of not liking who I was. I betrayed the possibility that I loved me. Instead, I hated me. I was an embarrassment to my dad. The last time I spoke to my dad before he passed, I apologized for the embarrassment I had been despite all he had invested in my life. All the years he tried to teach me how to be respectful. There's a story in the Bible about Balaam beating his donkey, and God spoke through the donkey and asked why Balaam was beating him. Balaam said the donkey was making a fool of him for lying down instead of doing what he was supposed to do. When God spoke through the donkey, He said, "Why have you beaten your donkey these three times? I have come here to oppose you because your path is a reckless one before me." Well, I was planning on going back to living the life I lived before and what I knew. I remember being in the visiting room in prison with Selena. We were sitting out there, and one of the therapists saw us. I had been in prisons so long all the personnel knew me, and I was on a first name basis with everybody. This therapist was Derry Glenn. I remember when Derry started out as a case manager and now, like Judge Doneghy, he was headed toward retirement. Derry is also City Councilman Glenn in Lima, Ohio. Back in 2009, though, when Derry saw me and Selena in the prison visiting room, he said, "Hey, Loomas (Derry always mispronounced my last name but I always let him), I like that girl there. She's different. It turned out everybody who saw me with Selena would say off the bat what a great person she was. Even the people who wanted dope from me told me to be good to Selena. They didn't want me to hurt that really nice lady I was with. Everybody kept telling me this during the nine months I served time, to not let Selena get away. Just like God talking through the donkey. I vowed that when my nine-month sentence was up, it was time for me to leave Toledo. When Selena came to pick me up at Allen Oakwood Correctional, I got in that car and went to Delta, Ohio, with her.

In the alley of the eastside of Toledo, making poor choices with my life.

My baby visiting me at Allen Correctional in 2009.
It's then that my life started to change and now here we are!

3

DELTA

I n 2009, Selena picked me up from prison and drove me to her hometown. At that time, Delta, Ohio, was about 96% white. There were some biracial kids, and then there was me. Selena and I weren't married. We lived in a small apartment in the country with Selena's youngest daughter, Destiny, who was 15. When I first met Selena, she used to party a little bit and worked in a nursing facility. People would come to Toledo to, for lack of better words, act bad. In the process of acting bad, Selena met me one day. For some reason, I was compelled to help her. I told her, "I'm going to help you get back to the country, but don't ever come back to the east side of Toledo again. It's not a place to play." Although she had lived on the east side a number of different times. She told me this wasn't her first rodeo. I told her it could be her last. We became friends. That's how our relationship started.

When I got home from the nine months in prison, I wasn't motivated to do much else other than stay at home, drink, and smoke weed. Selena and Destiny would go to church services on Wednesdays, and they would ask me to join them. I was looking for any excuse not to go. The irony was I got ordained in prison in 1988 in Lima Correctional. Inmates and convicts are highly skilled and highly intelligent. They figure out every kind of hustle there was. They have every tool in their arsenal to get ahead. Several older convicts told me if you're going to study the Bible and scripture, they recommended the Universal World Church study guide. They would ordain you if you passed a certain number of tests. In 1988 I was bored, so I went ahead and got the license. But in 2009, being ordained meant nothing to me. When I refused to go to church with Selena and Destiny at first, I told them it was because there is only one black person in that church, I know it was a mean thing to say, but I really did not want to go. Soon I settled on a better excuse. I started telling Selena and Destiny, "Well, God knows my number. If he wants me, he'll call me. Leave me alone. You pray for me, and I'll pray for you." This went on for about a month; every Wednesday and Sunday I would be drinking and smoking, they'd ask me to go to church, and I would throw out my excuse.

One Wednesday, in March of 2010, I gave Selena and Destiny my tired speech, "God knows my name, if he wants me, he'll call me. Tell him to call me". Well, off to church they went. I was outside in the country, smoking weed and drinking as usual. There was nothing or nobody out there.

You could hear the crickets. That was when I heard it, a voice as clear as day, and this is what I heard: "Your misfortune will be your fortune if you follow me." My first thought was, Get out of here! I must be smoking some bad weed. The voice came again, as clear as before: "Your misfortune will be your fortune if you follow me. The very thing you think makes you weak is your strength." This time, I stopped thinking to myself and started speaking to . . . that voice. I said, "I'm not scared of nothing. Do you know who I am?" Still not seeing anybody out there, I said, "I'm not really talking to God." The voice said, "Yes, I know exactly who you are." The voice then repeated, "If you follow me, your misfortune will be your fortune." I said, "Man, what about all the things I've done, the plagues I caused, and drugs I've sold, and all of that." The voice replied, "I know all about that. The very thing you think makes you weak is your strength. I had the feeling that I should go all in on the possibility that I was speaking to God. I said, "If you're God, then let's do this."

What happened next was nothing short of a miracle. I never drank again. I never smoked again. I suddenly couldn't hold any food down and could only drink just a little bit of water. I'd like to believe that God put me into a fast. I went to the doctor, and they thought it was just a virus. The next Wednesday, when Selena and Destiny got ready to go to church, I beat them to the car. Even though everyone else was excited I was finally going to church, I was scared. Before the lead worship singer could say, "Come to Jesus,"

I was drawn to the altar this time. I had practiced with all kinds of religions and studied with all kinds of people in prison without much effect. This time, in that church on that Wednesday in Delta, Ohio, I bawled. I left all of my shame and guilt there and didn't pick it up again. I felt liberated and free. I had this new lease on life because I was no longer carrying shame and guilt of ruining people's lives with drugs. I suddenly felt like I wanted my life to matter.

With this new energy and purpose, in 2010, I got on the computer and typed up a draft of my life. I wanted to talk about my past and the garbage because I wanted it gone. The best advice I got from the older convicts while I was serving time finally made sense to me. They would tell me, "Your life is your greatest asset. You only get one coin, so be careful how you spend it. Gangbanging is a high-risk activity, and it doesn't pay much, so you can either get better or bitter." I thought back to the scripture I had to learn when I was getting ordained decades before. I thought about Jeremiah 46:7 which says: "Who is this that rises up like the Nile, like the rivers in the delta of Egypt whose waters surge about?" As I sat there in Delta, Ohio, I made it my mission to only get better.

When I moved in on Circle Drive in Delta, Ohio 2009.

Me and my wife, Selena shortly after I was released from prison for the last time.

My wedding day. Here I am, marrying the love of my life and soulmate – Selena Lomas.

4

PLANTING SEEDS

I n one sense, I felt like I had become a new person. In another sense, I felt like some things hadn't changed. I still had no education except a prison GED and a vocational degree in accounting and computers, which I earned to stop from working in the prison kitchen. I knew how to type a little bit. I was at war with myself.

I had made a lot of money on the street, but I blew it all, so there wasn't anything piled in a vault waiting for me when I got out of prison. I lived for the day, so most of the money went to high priced criminal lawyers—they were the real pimps. Once that life gets you, it's hard to go back to being an ordinary person. Very few people get out with anything after doing the stuff I did. If you get out with your life, you're fortunate.

After I started going to church on a regular basis, I met Ron and Janet Broske. They were farmers who ran a successful greenhouse business in Delta. Ron came up to me and said, "I got a small farm out here, but I need a young man who is strong to be my assistant and help me out." I blurted out, "Whoa, man. I ain't that kind of Black guy. I'm from the city, I'm not from 1776! I don't know nothing about any farms." Ron might have grinned when he said, "No offense. I know you're Black. But I can tell you're a fine young man, and I want to help you in some kind of way." Realizing I had misread the situation, I took Ron up on his kind offer, went out, and became his assistant. I had gotten used to getting $18 a month in prison, and you'll be what they tell you you're going to be, or you'll sit in the hole. In other words, I was grateful for the work.

That job with Ron was no cakewalk. Even though he was 70, Ron was hands on and always right with you. I was scared to death when I saw him at his age getting up on that scaffold, talking non-stop while he was hanging the plants. His wife, Janet, was a sweetheart. Ron and Janet were very very humble. They were just good country people and enjoyed their lives as third or fourth generation farmers. They opened up a lot to me. I have to admit, it took getting used to people like Ron and Janet. As they got to know me and Selena better, when Ron and Janet would see me at church, Janet would pinch my face and tell Selena she was going to steal her husband. Later on, when Ron passed, Janet started to deteriorate mentally. She had been a real sharp lady. When they brought her to Ron's funeral, she didn't even realize that Ron had passed. It was a sad day. When I had that first encounter, God gave me Jesus 911,

I believed it was God's voice instructing me. It was like an old AM radio that we had in our bedroom as kids, and we tuned in to get old KCLW, which was the only station you could get blowing in from Detroit. Similarly, once I tuned into that "station" where I heard God, I was on a path and compelled to do these things. God told me to have a community ministry that resembled what Jesus and his disciples had, and it wasn't in a building. They were out in the community with ordinary people. Thinking about it, Jesus was probably the first social worker. My ministry, Jesus 911, was to be a church without walls. I wanted to be able to be out there, to be able to work with all people. I was just compelled to be thrusted into the community.

I got all gung-ho about the idea of Jesus 911. I met a guy named Jerry. I was telling him my vision to help the community and Jerry said, "You know what? I believe in you. Jerry gave me a space and off I went. Word spread about my positive spiritual services I had just birthed. People used to say, "Call 911 as fast as you can," when they were in trouble. People knew to call 911 due to the sense of urgency. If I'm in trouble I could say, "In the name of Jesus," and I'm immediately before the throne and have an advocate. So why would I try to dial 911 without consulting the person who has all the answers and can extend ultimate mercy and grace to anybody at any time? My message was that 911 is a man. I promoted making a conscious decision that something greater than you created you. That being has the ability to correct you. If you have computer software and you keep getting a warning that someone is trying to hack your system, it will eventually cause the computer to crash if you do nothing. Those hackers got that blueprint from the human anatomy. If we ignore what's going wrong, the system will shut down.

While I was working with Ron at the greenhouse and working my Jesus 911 ministry, I couldn't deny that something had changed in me. Reverting back to my old life wasn't going to be an option. I couldn't call somebody to get a shipment of cocaine anymore. I had come to the realization that I no longer could do the things that I used to do after that encounter with God. I had a moral compass that had kicked in. Funny enough, my former associates did call me when I got out of prison. I went to my connection's house because my son's grandmother (she had raised my oldest two kids while I was out living my so-called "best life") had passed, so I wanted to get some clothes for my son, my daughter, and me to look presentable for the funeral. When I got there, it seemed like everybody from my past was there. There was something else there, too: A half a key of cocaine and a phone sitting on the table. While I stared at all that, my connection said, "There you go, man. You know we got your back." I said, "No, man, I just want some money for a suit." There was silence. Then my connection yelled out, "I won the bet! I told you that dude was done!" He had a

$1,000 bet I wouldn't take the drugs and the phone. That

was as close as I came to ever being involved in my old life again.

I was involved as a serial trafficker for a long time. I trafficked anything I could get my hands on, whether it was stolen goods or drugs. I then learned that I didn't need to have drugs, I just needed to know where to get them from and broker the deal. That made me valuable and irreplaceable because of what I knew. As fate would have it, all the people I was indebted to either got life in prison, the death penalty, or were murdered. Their kids and relatives tried to approach me when I got out of my last prison stint, but then they just let me go. When they saw I was serious about helping people, they started to support me. They actually followed me and encouraged me. Former customers who I thought would never forgive me were my biggest supporters.

Even though I was ordained by Universal Life Church back in 1988, I did not do any counseling when I was in prison. When I started Jesus 911 in 2010, I called Universal Life Church out of the blue to check on my status. The people who had ordained me at Universal Life Church had passed on, but their kids checked the old register and I was still in good standing. I went and registered in Ohio and Tennessee to make everything legitimate about Jesus 911. One day, during a Jesus 911 meeting, I was ministering to a lady. She seemed to respond to me and what I was doing so she said to me, "Why don't you call the Ridge Project?

Their executive director is an anointed man, and he helps people who are in and out of prison. They also have one of the largest fatherhood initiative programs in the country. You would be a big help to them." She also mentioned that my story sounded a lot like the story of the founder and executive director of the organization. Now, I had never heard of the Ridge Project. But I had learned by this time not to ignore a message when I heard one. So I said, "Why not?"

5

RIDGE PROJECT

I called the receptionist at the Ridge Project, who was a friend of the lady who referred me to the organization. She said they were doing some hiring, and she gave me a preliminary interview over the phone. Then she invited me in for a more formal "three-step" interview. I had no clue what a three-step interview was, but I was about to find out.

The Ridge Project was based in Defiance, Ohio. After I drove over there for the first interview, they had me take personality tests. I was told that the owners of the Ridge Project believed that those tests would reveal if I would be a fit in the organization. The results of my test indicated I was a "dazzling diplomat." Like my father, I never met a stranger. For the second interview, I was waiting around with about 20 other candidates, who were well dressed and had bachelor's degrees and master's degrees. There I was with my prison GED wearing a secondhand suit I got from one of the brothers at the church. At that moment, I really had no confidence. All I had going for me was my personality and my past. That was either going to kill me or make me.

While I was waiting for my interview, a short Latino man in an expensively tailored suit and a woman walk into the office. The Latino man was upset. He then explained he was upset because they had missed their flight. He passed by, went into his office, and slammed his door. I thought nothing of it. A second later, the door opens, the Latino man walks out, looks at me and says, "Hey, Robbie! It's me!" I look at this guy like, "Who are you?" He said, "It's Ron. I had the cell next door to you at Lima Correctional! We played in the band together!" Well, talk about a shocker. The Ridge Project was owned and run by my old friend Ron Tijerina and his wife, Cathy. The other candidates for the job looked like, "We might as well go home, we know who's got this job." I didn't recognize Ron because the last time I saw him we were wearing blue prison shirts with numbers on them, like Clint Eastwood did in Escape From Alcatraz. If Ron was wearing that outfit, I would've recognized him quicker! When I first met Ron, he had just been transferred from Lucasville, which was one of the harder prisons. I was playing the guitar I got on loan from the prison chapel. Ron comes over to me and asks, "Hey, who taught you to play Spanish guitar?" I said, "Nobody taught me to play Spanish guitar. I just heard it." Ron looks at me and said, "What do you mean, you 'heard it'?" I told Ron, "I never had a lesson in my life—if I hear it, I can play it." It was true. When I was younger, I just thought I could play it. Ron said, "We got a band, so why don't you come up to the chapel? We really need a guitar player." I go up there, and nobody spoke English except Ron. He joked with me and said, "Rob, you have a Spanish-sounding last name so you'll fit right in." So I jammed with the Latinos and worked through the broken English, and soon enough, we had a jazz band going.

Ron's cell was next to mine, and I would hear him typing all the time. Ron was a Bible-thumper who was serving 16 years for a crime he didn't commit. He wanted nothing to do with anything that was wrong in prison because he was innocent, and he didn't belong there. Everybody's innocent in prison, by the way. I asked Ron one day, while I was smoking some weed and was high, "TJ, what are you doing?" (We couldn't pronounce Ron's last name of "Tijerina," so we just called him TJ.) Ron told me, "God has given me and my wife Cathy a vision so that when I get out of here, we're going to help families get healed. We're working on a curriculum that is going to heal communities and liberate men all across the country." I spit my hooch out laughing at him. I didn't take Ron, let alone visions, too seriously back in 2003. Ron and I soon went our separate ways; I was sent to Belmont Correctional, and Ron was shipped to North Central Correctional. As a result, we lost contact with each other over the years. In 2010, Ron was the executive director of that vision. His curriculum is taught all over the world for re-entry into society. He and Cathy speak all over the world and write books. Now Ron was in a position to hire me. He jabbed me by saying, "Remember when you used to make fun of me about what I was working on? Here it is!" Who was laughing now?

Ron asked me to come into his office, and I followed him in there. Sure enough, he had a guitar, and we sang some old tunes from our prison band days. Ron's wife, Cathy, came in, introductions were made, then she said, "OK, we have to grow up and hire somebody now." They had a policy to not hire anybody that Ron served time with, but they bent the rules for me. I could barely type or do anything else, but my new supervisor, Chris Pierce, trained me. Chris was a former Assemblies of God pastor. Pastor Chris was an amazing grant writer, and I learned a lot from him very quickly.

One of my jobs at The Ridge Project was to teach fatherhood initiatives to inmates in prison. I would come into the institutions and teach classes about how to be a father. It was a struggle at first. I had anxiety going back to prison, walking through the gate with a suit on—going back through the gate, period. I had to get shook down again and all of that. It also took me getting pointers from Pastor Chris about handling large groups. Sometimes we would have between 50 and 60 prisoners in the group. We would go through a lot of training to learn how not to lose control because you are dealing with hardened inmates. I knew that from being inside, that they could sense your fear. I came up with a strategy for handling that. After the third day of a group session, I would say to them, "If any of these things don't mean anything to you, like being a better son for your mom, or being a better neighbor, or being a better father for your kids, if that's not you, please get up and leave. I'll give you some free envelopes or free pens or some other stuff, and you come back when you're man enough to take this class because this is a grown man class, it's not a baby class. No bottles are going to be passed out here." That approach won me some respect. Some inmates would get up, shake my hand in appreciation and say, "Thanks, but my mind is somewhere else. Can I come back later on?

As part of my training, I got sent to Golden, Colorado, a place which I had never heard of. The Ridge Project wanted married people to go there and have couples training and get certified. I met with Phyllis and Sherod Miller. They were old hippies who were professors, and they had developed communication curriculum in the '70s. They trained organizations all over. I went out there, and they left out something from the fine print: I would be teaching the curriculum to lifers and their wives. The material as they crafted it was a tough sell to my unique audience. I, again, learned how to put my twist on it, though. One of the things that I promoted for a healthy marriage and relationship was that you should give your significant other 100% and expect nothing in return and vice versa, instead of keeping score. I practice that to this day with my wife, Selena. As a result, she's happy when I'm happy.

Once I got back to The Ridge Project in Ohio, I set up my

routine. Typically, I would be in the office at 5 a.m., picking up books and curriculum. I would usually arrive at the Marion Correctional Institution at 8 a.m. If it was a marriage/couples communication class we would bring the wives in, which meant I had to make sure they weren't smuggling anything in. Even though I took that precaution, I didn't want a guard in the classroom that would make the inmates feel uncomfortable. Then there was the issue that a lot of men don't realize: women don't see things from the same perspective. I had to teach that men can't get upset about that. Men had to take this into consideration: Do I want to be right at the expense of making my wife feel belittled or making her feel bad? I also made it a habit to not counsel while sitting across a desk. My intent with that dynamic was to make sure there wasn't a feeling of separation. I didn't want anybody to feel like a broken person - only a person. A lot of times other therapists I worked with didn't understand that the nonverbals communicate a lot to somebody. Those therapists made people feel like, "I'm here to fix you, broken little man." A person is already low enough, so I took all of that away.

I worked with child support services and judges in every town. I worked as an advocate for people in prison and on parole. I knew more about the thought process of an inmate than someone who had more schooling because I had lived it. I could make the adjustments in an approach quickly. I could say, "I've been there and done that. You're not going to beat the system like that." Because of my background I could call people out without them being offended.

When I wear a hat that says "Man of Faith," where do you think I got that faith from? In prison! As a prisoner, I couldn't see over that wall, so I had to believe that something was going to happen eventually. I got it because I had to navigate the minefields of prison. One thing I learned from old timers in prison. They used to say, "You got to think for a fool as well as yourself cause you never know what a crazy guy is going to do in prison." They got that right. When I was in prison, to say it wasn't safe was an understatement. There was no "unit management." Everybody had to make weapons. One brutal weapon guys made was to take Magic Shave that Black guys used, they would add some powder, urine, and feces in it and then let it sit for days. When someone wanted to inflict some serious damage, they would throw that concoction in someone's face, and the acid would melt the victim's face off. I had seen plenty of people get killed. They would cry for their mama and say that they were seeing things as they died. People work out so much in prison because they want to be better able to survive a piping or a stabbing. Odds were against surviving most attacks. If someone got stabbed and their guts were hanging out, they still have to wait to be shackled in order to get transported to the hospital. Too much time would be taken up to shackle a stabbed inmate. It was a surprise if someone got shanked and came back alive. Sometimes the guards would kill you.

They were more dangerous back then than the people you did time with. Absolute power corrupts people, and those guards had the power over the prisoners. Most of the prisons are in rural towns. It was a common story: A guy had dreams and hopes and then had to settle for working in a prison. Those guards were bitter for being stuck where they were. The result was a recipe for disaster: A part time KKK member and survivalist guard vs. criminals. Prisoners were not used to taking orders from anybody, and that was why they get beaten to death. Prisoners also have no contact with anybody. When I first got there, I found that women stayed faithful to their husbands. While Ron was incarcerated, his wife, Cathy and his kids were practically raised in the visitor room in prison. Women waited years for their husbands. I was (and continue to be) impressed with how hard relationships were worked at.

Another thing I knew about my audience was that men who did longer hard time were less likely to reoffend than someone who did 18 months. Once those things are taken away from you, like the ability to get a cold drink or take a walk in the park, you learn to appreciate the simple things. You can leave prison one of two ways: Either bitter or better. When I was visiting in Hocking Hills, I went to see an old friend, who was an ex-Marine. He was the real deal; he jumped out of planes and fought in Desert Storm. I used to sell him cocaine for him and his soldiers when he was on the base. He said something to me when I was serving time in Lima in 2003. I said, "Man, I can't wait until I get out. Do you know how good and kind I've been to everybody?" He is there smoking his cigarette, and he says, "Rob, can I say something to you? We both go back a long ways, we both come from the country, so I'm gonna say this to you." I said, "Go ahead, say whatever you want to say." He said, "Rob, you were not a nice person. You were a heartless drug dealer and a pimp." I thought he was going to say something nice! He said, "Someone needs to tell you the truth. You were not a role model citizen. You were here because you belonged here. You got a good heart, but you were heartless at times." He said I had lost my way and had to check myself. I was a dangerous person on the street. I was a cancer in the community. The people who looked up to me were dead or locked up. I thought I was right when I was living that life. We were shooting it out with AKs in projects over drug turf disputes. We didn't see it as anything other than life as usual. We couldn't be bullied; we had to hold our own.

My former life, rough as it was, gave me the perspective to see myself in others and help those who needed saving from themselves. As a result of my unique perspective, my reputation grew. What I also soon discovered was that corporate America is more treacherous than the drug trade! Only difference is they use a pen. Some people didn't like it when me and Ron got together because we were treated almost like royalty when we went back to the prison and jammed with the band there. We knew everybody. Even though Ron was a big deal now and spoke all over the world, with me, he was just TJ.

When I worked for Ron and Cathy, I was a case manager, facilitator, and re-entry guide. I had been in the system, but there were employees who had never been in the system. I can recall one particular incident when a guy who didn't have a background was teaching a class at Toledo Correctional, the guys in there would give him a hard time. They acted stupid and said, "What do you know?" They were really going at it, trying to intimidate him. But this facilitator wasn't having any of it. I'll never forget what he told the inmates. He said, "Can I say something to you gentlemen? You know what, I've never been in jail. I've always been a church boy, and I was always the apple of Grandmama's eye. But I'm going to tell you something. What I can tell you is how to hold a job, how to love people, how to treat your neighbor next door. I could show you how to respect yourself and be a good dad. Does that stand for anything?" The facilitator then said, "I'm here because I love you, and you're going to be coming back to my community. I want you to be the best version of you that you can be and make sure you have all the tools to be successful.

People had to understand I had served time in so many prisons they couldn't send me into a prison I didn't know somebody, whether they were White, Black, Mexican, or Other. So, when I came into the yard I was like a rock star. People in packs and droves would say, "Rob, help me, help me. Could you call the judge, could you do this, could you do that? You know what it's like to be in here, man. Could you write my wife?" Even the guards wanted to talk to me. People who worked with me got tired of this and ended up saying they couldn't work with me. My credibility was a benefit and a burden. When I sold drugs on the street, people sought out my advice because they thought I had all the answers. I believe there's always a solution to every problem. The Rob Lomas way was, and still is, the A, B, C plan. And if all else fails, never quit. That came from my upbringing, not the streets. My dad grew up in the Jim Crow South, and he didn't use that hardship as a crutch, he used it as a strength. He said, "If I could pick cotton and chop sugarcane since I was a little boy and make it all the way here, what's impossible?" I watched my dad's journey and my mom's journey, so I never quit or gave up. I was writing letters for men who were up for parole to support them. One day, a lady from Child Support came to me and said, "I saw the letter you wrote, and I really wish you wouldn't send this to the judge." I couldn't believe it. I told her, "That was that guy's mail, and you shouldn't have opened it up." She said, "We're from Lima, and we don't believe that guy is the person you say he is." I said, "I'm just telling it like it is from what I see in my classroom. Besides that, it's against the law for you to be opening up that man's mail." She didn't seem to care and threatened me with, "If you send this letter, you're gonna be sorry." That's when two guys warned me that the education room that Child Support in Allen County was letting me use was bugged and wired. That's how they knew what we talked about in that room. They played back the recordings for me, and I felt betrayed. Some of the things shared in there were supposed to be private. For example, we had an exercise called the "mirror exercise." We took a small vanity mirror and built a circle of chairs around a guy. Once we get to a point in the fatherhood curriculum, the facilitator gives a guy a mirror and the guy has to tell his story to himself. All the other guys do at that point is support and encourage him, but the guy can't talk to anyone else. Some guys get talking to that mirror and start bawling their eyes out as they share how they were molested, or they rape people in prison because they were raped at home. Child Support knew we did those exercises, and for them to record them and play them back to use against a guy, that was horrible. They twisted a guy's story around completely. What happened next was a powerful supervisor from child support tells Ron that, "Rob is a great guy, but he's a male chauvinist, and he was arrogant. He was a kingpin, and he was used to people kissing up to him." She was accusing me of having people kiss my ring to get things done. Ron called me in for a warning.

A few months later, I was teaching a class, and Chris told me they wanted me back at the main office. He told me to not even finish the class. So I go back there, and they told me they wanted to agree to part ways with me. I had a dream a week before. That's how I get my visions. For example, earlier in the year I told Ron I had a dream he was going to Washington D.C. and that, "Y'all going to be invited by Obama's administration to speak. But Ron, you won't be able to get in, and you will be walking back to the hotel carrying a brown paper." Ron did get invited to D.C., and he couldn't get in because he was a convicted felon. I had another dream that TJ was yelling at me. When I returned to the Ridge Project office, I was questioned about some paperwork complaints. We agreed to part ways. Lima organizations are mostly run by strong women. They wanted me put in my place. We agreed to part ways. I asked them to pray with me, and then I left. I had been a facilitator with Ron and Cathy at Ridge Project for a year. I valued my time there, I was grateful for the opportunity, and learned many valuable lessons. I learned to always know your worth. I learned the five Ps: Proper Preparation Prevents Poor Performance. I learned when speaking to always know your audience. I learned the Ridge Project model, and what it means to be a Tyro Dad. Finally, the Tijerinas not only educated me about the workings of corporate America but also allowed me to gain confidence in my untapped skills. By the time I left Ridge Project in 2013, I was a certified couples communication instructor, a certified fatherhood facilitator, and a re-entry coordinator. Now I had to use my new skills and credentials to land on my feet again.

6

RENEWED

At first, I was very hurt and confused after parting ways with the Ridge Project because God had shown me favor and had been blessing everything I put my hands on. I had faith that I was being called on to do other work. After the split with Ron and Cathy, I became a volunteer chaplain at Cherry Street Missions in Toledo. I also was a volunteer chaplain at Toledo Gospel Rescue Mission. However, those were tough times because we became dependent on the bonuses and salary the Ridge Project provided. Even though my wife, Selena, worked as a home health aide, our family survived on our faith and generous support of our Christian brothers and sisters.

My next job was at the Volunteers of America (also known as VOA) at a halfway house in Toledo. It was a place I knew all too well; I had stayed there six months in 2004 on a furlough after completing my seven-and-a-half-year prison sentence for possession of cocaine. I was responsible for making rounds and checking on the residents living in the house. I would have to give the men random urine tests and check them in and out of the building for work assignments. It was surreal working at a place I used to sleep at. Only God could do that. I worked there for almost a year, and during that time, I was still volunteering at the Cherry Street Mission through my Jesus 911 Community Ministries. I was driving back and forth from Wauseon to Toledo, a 45 minute commute each way. Working at the VOA was a great fit for my skill set because these were my people, and we spoke the same language. These were men coming home from prison sentences and trying their best not to succumb to their demons. I knew their thoughts and could intervene before they could act on them. I recall one exchange with a young gangbanger. He said to me, "What do you know about doing time?" I said matter-of-factly, "Just so happened I served a little time before." He scoffed and said, "What, like, seven days in the county?" I replied, "No, seven years in prison. And, oh, I used to sleep right over there." The young man still didn't get it and said, "Over on that side of town?" I said, "No, that bed next to yours." He was shocked! It did not take long for the word to get back to my supervisor that he had hired a guy that used to be a resident there. He called me into his office and said to me, "I thought your face looked familiar." I said, "I thought you knew who I was." He just said keep up the good work.

In 2014, I was reading the paper one morning when I got off work at VOA and stumbled across a help wanted ad that read "Monitor Wanted: Competitive Wage." So, I called the Fresh Start Dual Diagnosis Treatment Center, which was part of Recovery Services, and asked what the job requirements were. I was then put through to Earl Grant, who was the program director at the time. Earl was a trauma therapist who used to be a crack addict. He got clean at Fresh Start, went back to school, and became the director there. When I told Earl I was currently employed at the VOA he asked me out for an interview. Before Earl got off the phone with me, he asked if I was Black, and I replied, "The last time I checked!" He said, "I'm just asking because there are not many Black guys living in Fulton County, and I thought I knew all of them."

The Fresh Start/Recovery Services treatment center was in a small farming village called Alvordton. The town did not have a police station, a store, or a gas station. However, it did have a bar right across the street from the rehab center. How convenient for the patients if they relapsed to go right across the street to order a drink at the bar. Or they could go right down the street to see the local meth dealer. I was able to successfully use my skills at Fresh Start/Recovery Services that I honed while working at Ridge Project. My job was similar to what I was doing at the VOA. Earl hired me as his monitor and instructed me to feel free to use a heavy hand to restore order back into place because he couldn't be everywhere. The guy who was my supervisor was a man of high character and morals named Doug Stirtz. One of my responsibilities was to drive the guys to their Narcotics Anonymous or Alcoholics Anonymous meetings. I would often have the opportunity to speak with the clients during the long commutes. One day, a young therapist named Matt called me into his office. He said, "Rob, I am amazed by you. You tell all the guys the right thing to do. I can't believe that you don't have any formal training. Have you ever thought about going back to school?" I laughed and scoffed, "I am too old." That's when Earl, who had overheard us, popped his head and said, "You are never too old." Both of them then went to work on me and told me if I didn't go back to school, I would be missing my calling. After that conversation, I started taking chemical dependency assistance courses.

I also worked with several strong women at the treatment center. We had Crystal, who was the lead substance abuse counselor. Crystal taught me how to better control the group and the importance, at times, of staying on topic. We were also blessed with Jean. Jean was a former hairdresser and banker, who then became a certified substance abuse counselor. Jean worked with us as a volunteer counselor, case manager, and driver and also did whatever else was needed. Jean never made a dime for the time she spent working with men and women in recovery. We also had Jesse and Marie, who were the case managers. Earl, Matt, Crystal, and I worked in recovery. The term "recovery" meant we were all former alcoholics and addicts living clean and were actively involved in a 12-step program.

Unfortunately, the office politics that I experienced at Ridge Project came back to haunt me at Fresh Start/Recovery Services. Even though it was a faith-based organization, spiritual jealousy ran rampant. Like my dad, I never met a stranger, and I got along with everybody. I could talk about anything with anybody. If someone wanted to talk Bob Seger or The Beatles or Otis Redding or James Brown, so be it. I could go to the Country Music Hall of Fame and be right at home with Buck Owens and Hank Williams. After a while, other facilitators and counselors would become jealous. It was like Joseph when he was sold into slavery after he told his brothers about his dream. If you want the Joseph favor, you're going to get what Joseph got. You've got to take the crushing of the grapes if you want the sweet taste of the wine. Other people were jealous of the results I got working with others. They felt threatened by my gifts of being able to connect with people, so they feared me.

Not long after I started working there, Recovery Services sold its in-patient men's treatment center to a company called Renewed Mind. Renewed Mind leased the current office space from Recovery Services. They also announced that the current staff could stay in place but would be running open interviews for several positions. We were promised financial incentives, and the new leadership seemed to be much laxer than Recovery Services. There was still some resentment toward me from other employees because of how effective I was at my job.

On February 18th, 2015, a bad winter storm had hit. Our blessed Jean was driving our clients Matt and Jeremy to the emergency room because they had the flu. Matt was a Marine from Desert Storm. He had been shot and became addicted to painkillers. Matt was an ex-basketball player, and we would always talk about sports. When I was working in the center, he would always ask me what the score of this game or that game was. Jean thought she could safely make the drive because the road had been cleared. As Jean was driving on US20 near US127 west of Fayette, she lost control of the Chevrolet Cavalier she was driving, crossed the centerline, and collided with a van. The driver of the van was, coincidentally, delivering vegetables to our center. Tragically, Jean died in the emergency room of St. Luke's Hospital from her injuries, and Matt and Jeremy were sent to Toledo. Jean had left the center at 11 a.m., and when 4 p.m. rolled around and she wasn't back, people got worried. Earl was talking to Matt , and he said he had seen a bad accident up the road on his way back from a woman's treatment center. He didn't even recognize that it was Jean's car because it was so badly mangled. A state trooper arrived at the center during a group meeting that afternoon. He had Jean's purse, said she was involved in a car accident and that she didn't make it. There wasn't a dry eye in that center. Jean's car sat out there at the accident site for a couple of weeks before her husband could get it because he was traumatized. Every time we went by Jean's car we cried because we knew she was dead and not coming to work. I will never forget Jean's smile, her willingness to be of service to others, or her willingness to give of her time to those less fortunate. May she rest well, faithful servant.

Not long after Jean's passing, I came into work for my second shift. I learned that they were going to pull the plug on Matt because he wasn't improving from the injuries he suffered in the accident. Matt's mother wanted us to go to the hospital to say goodbye. During this emotional time, once again corporate America reared its ugly head (remember, it does more damage with a pen than a gun). I was at that moment told I had to stay behind. After I told them I wanted to say goodbye to Matt, I was told I instead had to talk to Ryan, who was the head director at Renewed Mind (Earl Grant had stayed with the Recovery Services division). Not seeing what was coming, I meet with Ryan and the program director. They told me I had lied on my employment application, and they were going to fire me. They said, "We believe that you have been involved with some horrible crimes in the past, and we don't think it's appropriate that you are working here. We thought you had sold a little bit of drugs in the past, but we didn't know you were a big-time supplier. It's not a good look for the company." I was devastated, but the bad day didn't end there. They continued to treat me like I was a dirty criminal, and I couldn't go in and get my belongings. I was being totally judged by my past. Like I've said, spiritual jealousy runs rampant. Even though the 10th commandment says, "Thou shall not covet," that I shouldn't be looking at your life and become envious, coveting is what made these people rise up against me. Just like in the Bible, Joseph's brothers were jealous of Joseph's gifts, so they sold him into slavery. I later discovered that one of the people who was allegedly behind my firing was the very person who had encouraged me to go back to school.

My unjustified firing from Renewed Mind just confirmed to me that people fear what they can't understand. The people I worked with couldn't understand why I could effectively reach people when they couldn't. If they looked closer, they'd see I've earned the right because I had walked in the clients' shoes to come straight in the front door at them. When I led group sessions, I would say, "If I'm not at your door, I'm in your neighborhood when you're making up excuses to give up on life." In other words, no one in group could ever say to me, "Yo, Rob, you ain't never been to prison, or you ain't never done time, or you ain't never done dope, or you ain't never carried a gun, or you ain't never shot nobody." I've shot and been shot at. Next. I can say to anyone at any time, "I've got 27 felonies, would you like to borrow some? I got seven prison numbers. I'm Black and I'm old, and I'm working and I'm getting my education, what's your excuse? I don't want to hear any excuses. I need you to pick up your cross and bear it, brother." I could say that to people straight up, and other counselors couldn't say that. I tried to tell the others I worked with about not having the desk separating them from the clients because it was like they were looking down at them, reminding them of their brokenness and their flaws. But the other therapists didn't want to hear about my thoughts on that.

There was a time when I used to make so much money a day just roaming around drunk. Everybody owed me money. It got to the point where I was tired of counting money. I eventually learned humility. One of the best pieces of advice I got was from Derry Glenn, a city councilman of Lima, who was my therapist. He said, mispronouncing my name as he usually did, "Loomas, learn everything you can by doing." I thought I had moved on from my past. But do you really ever move on from your past bad decisions? I learned over the years that not only is it important to take ownership of all choices you make but to stand by them. I learned that if you don't tell your story, somebody else will tell it for you, and it's a safe bet it won't be your account that's being told. I believe that not coming to terms with your past can not only affect your present but also can rob you of your future. I've learned that my past has not defined my future; however, it has qualified me for my higher calling by observing God well for my life and mankind.

After being fired, I came home. I was still shocked by it. On the second day of being home, Doug Stirtz, who had trained me, came by my house to tell me he had resigned. He said he was my Christian brother (he was white) and that he couldn't work for a place that treated me so badly. "If you go, I go. I can't work at a place like that," Doug told me. Now, Doug did not have it easy; he had to work an extra job to pay for caring for his daughter, who was diabetic. I was really shocked now because Doug quit a job out of principle and for a Black guy. Talk about a high-character dude.

Doug even went a step further and suggested I contact lawyers at the Ohio Civil Rights Service office in Toledo. Doug advised me to complain of workplace discrimination against me by Renewed Mind. He backed me up and told the lawyers there that I was fired because a therapist was jealous of me and pulled rank on me because I wasn't licensed. It turns out Renewed Mind then hired a guy who was younger than me, so it also became the basis for an age discrimination case. I could have made it about race since I was the only Black therapist there, but I didn't do that. What ended up happening was that Renewed Mind had to reinstate me as a counselor and give me back pay. They had tried to pay me an extra $10,000 to be quiet and go away, but I knew God put me there for a reason, so I was going to fight to stay there. I saw how guys lit up with hope when I talked to them and helped them. They saw I used to be them, and now I was employed. It instilled hope in them, even when I was just driving them to a meeting. I had to stay the course and keep breaking down doors for all the other formerly incarcerated individuals trying to forge their way back into productive law-abiding citizens.

My wife told me, "You already won because you changed."

When I came back to work at Renewed Mind, everyone was shocked. I shook everybody's hand and went back to what I was doing. I got wind of the fact they were going to fire the man they hired to replace me, so I stepped in. I said, "No, keep him as a counselor, he's a fine young man. I'll be a monitor (they had been ordered to rehire me as a counselor), and I'll keep going to school." They waited for me to act like I was rubbing their wrongdoing in their faces, but I went on like nothing had happen. I wanted them to see what forgiveness and love means. What we were doing at the organization was not about us, it was about these individuals who were trying to hold on for dear life. I held on with Renewed Mind for another five years, until I left in 2020.

7

HIGHER LEARNING

While pursuing the formal education I wanted and needed, I went through the state of Ohio and took courses online. I studied at Argosy University to get my B.A. in psychology. When I was working at the center and things got somewhat quiet, I took out my laptop and did my schoolwork. It turned out my years on the street and then in the workplace had prepared me for school. Everything we were doing in the courses, I was already doing in the treatment center. The methods I was employing at the treatment center were based on my experience on the streets and in prison. For the things I wasn't schooled in already, I could pick the brain of the social workers and therapists at the center because I'm right there. At the same time, I'm educating them about the stuff I had lived.

At the treatment center we met every Wednesday for staffing. They would give us coffee and donuts, and we would staff all of the clients. They used to call the clients in to answer for their foolishness and stumbling blocks that's stopping them from getting to the next phase of their recovery. When I saw them constantly trying to divide mental health and substance abuse, I started seeing things differently because I had lived it. I knew that mental health issues stem from trauma. All substance abuse stems from trauma, in my opinion. Trauma is the gateway drug. I don't believe marijuana and beer is a gateway drug, trauma is. That trauma is what interrupts you and diverts you. I stand by the theory that people get high for one of two reasons: To feel something, or to forget something. As I would explain to my groups, "I'm dealing with something that's too painful for me to remember, so either I suppress the memory like it never happened, or I start masking it with other things. Sex, drugs, alcohol, or something else. I feel unattractive, but when I get high, I feel beautiful. I'm shy when I'm not drinking, but I'm not shy when I do, like when people say you're a whole other person after a couple of drinks." This had happened to me, and I had finally recognized it.

Based on my own hard knocks, I started to simplify things when I was helping others. I figured that treatment did not need to be so complicated. One of the many things I learned from Ron Tijerina was to always know your audience. I broke it down to always know who I'm working with. We are not all the same, we're all unique individuals. To put the person in their best position to succeed or to discover what's really ailing them, I'd rather speak to them about what's wrong, rather than the obvious. Like I tell my groups, "Alcohol didn't do anything to you, it's your intent behind you using it." People who have been programmed to talk about 12 steps get mad at me. They make alcohol and drugs the devils. The problem you can't face is the issue. I target the issue. They would call me the anti-12 step guy at the treatment center. It's not my intent to flat out bash it, but instead, I'm promoting the step of conscious decision. Before we can do anything else, hope must be restored. I learned that when I worked with Cherry Street Mission. We had guys coming in and they had been out on the street for years. Their immediate concern was shelter and food. I couldn't talk to them about getting a job right off the bat. They weren't in shape for finding a job, let alone keeping one. I saw that people in mental health, even with all of their degrees, put the cart before the horse because they were more concerned about the system. Even before I began getting my degrees, my uniqueness was that I was the former king of chaos, so I could talk to the worst of the worst and give them hope. When I was out there in the streets, I was the ringleader with the clowns and bears, and I could handle the circus. I smoked a joint, did a double shot of some brown liquor or Jim Beam, and I was ready to go. I used to tell the police, "You got a job to do, and so do I." In the streets, my discernment was a gift from God and if I make the wrong call about a guy, it costs me my life. I had to be able to read people, and read them well and quick. When

I was finally dealing with clients in treatment, I would tell them, "I can actually see you, and whatever you're selling, I'm not buying. I'm here because I want to help you. I want to turn the mess into a message. I don't want you to go through what I went through." I wasn't blowing smoke. I controlled the east side of Toledo for the drug trade. I had gangsters working for me, of all races. The Black guys were mad at me for having employees of other races. People would come to me with their problems because I was a leader, and I answered to nobody on the street. That's probably where I got a foundation in helping me talk to people in treatment because they wanted answers and solutions. I was used to getting the best out of people and their talents. I had a track record for getting the best out of people. Of course, the time came where I needed to get the best out of my best self, too. When I got off the streets and out of prison, I prayed and asked God one day, "God, show me how to get the confidence that I once had in a way that is useful and helpful." When people seek me out, they are on their last legs, and they expect to be helped. The biggest challenge I had in school was APA format and citation. Not to point out the obvious, but I didn't grow up using that. I only failed one class by a percentage point because of a citation error. The professor was an Argosy alumnus too. That pissed me off. It was a community counseling class, and she thought I didn't take her class seriously. I went from there to get my masters. I earned my bachelor's degree in psychology in four years. I was invited to Nashville for the graduation ceremony. While I was in the Music City Hall receiving my degree, I thought how surreal it all was. I had tried to go to school at South University back when I worked at the Ridge Project, but it didn't go well. After I earned my bachelor's degree, I went on with Argosy to get my masters. I also got my CDCA (Chemical Dependency Assistance License). I am a LICDC. I had come a long way, but as it turned out, I had many other roads left to travel.

Receiving my bachelor's degree in Nashville, Tennessee from Argosy University.

My wife and I after receiving my Master's Degree in Forensics Psychology in Nashville, Tennessee.

Masters Degree

8

HUMBLE SERVANT, TOUGH LOVE

One of my mentors was Pastor Randy Trowbridge. He mentored me when I first accepted my calling at Delta Assembly of God, and he had been the local pastor, along with his wife, Kathy. I accepted the calling, and God sent me to a 99% predominantly European church, and that was where I was supposed to be. My excuse for not going to the local church was that there wasn't but one local Black lady, We all are a little prejudiced; I'm not talking about racial prejudice but rather our inclination to prejudge anything. We all prejudge. We all are guilty of that at some point in our life. People took the word and made it into something else. When I used to teach communication classes, Sherod Miller used to say if you meet a person the first time and they leave you with a bad impression, it will take 25 more encounters to change your mind. You want to hit a home run the first time, so that is why I always try to bring my A game.

When I got myself together after being released from

prison for the last time, I went to Delta. I was drawn there by the spirit, and I shared with Pastor Randy what had happened to me. I was the first interracial marriage he ever performed, since there were no other Black people in town. He taught me that I should never marry anyone without pre-marriage counseling. A feather could have knocked him over when he found out I was a licensed minister. I told him I had to do a funeral and he said, "You mean you have to speak at a funeral?" You had to be licensed and ordained to officiate a funeral, and I had been one since 1988. Pastor Randy looked at my degree and said, "I guess you can do anything I do."

My cousin, Carmelita, is 10 years older than me. She was a head cook at the Inverness Golf Club for almost 30 years. She retired, and five months later, she was shopping when her head started hurting. They took her to St. Vincent Hospital, and she tells her husband (my cousin, Tyronne), "You go home, go to work. I'll be all right." She slipped into a coma, and three days later, she was taken off life support and died. My younger cousin, who looked up to me, said, "You know, Mama wanted you to do her funeral." I said, "I can't do that. I'm not ready, I'm not prepared." She looked at me and rolled her eyes (she was a nurse), and she said to me, "The same way you found the guts to walk through those prisons and do all that time, and the same way you huffed and puffed around those streets is the same way you're gonna do my mother's funeral. I'll see you there." There was no arguing with her after that. Still, I was a nervous wreck. Keep in mind, I had to return to Toledo, Ohio. Many of the people did not know "Reverend Rob" or "Minister Rob," and they did not know about my conversion.

When the day of the funeral arrived, it was not just any funeral—it was a mega funeral. Carmelita knew all kinds of people from all walks of life. I could not believe I was responsible for officiating this large of a crowd. It was my first funeral, and I felt like I was in an Abbott and Costello skit, when they're scared to death and their knees were knocking together. I was shaking just like that. I had a friend who I was in prison with named Myron, whose nickname was Maestro. He had recorded music all over. Myron had got out, so I called him and asked him to handle the music for me. He said, "I'll stand up there with you, brother. I knew your cousin." Him being there relaxed me. I also got some pointers before the funeral. For example, once you remember that everybody is here to see you, no one will know if you messed up or not. Crack a corny joke and keep on going. The only way they'll know if you messed up is if you stop. I was the Pastor, and everybody was looking to me to keep it flowing. A friend of mine called and she asked me if I would officiate her son's wedding. It was an outdoor wedding at a huge house in the country, with a large pond and a boat deck. The wedding was Hawaiian themed, complete with a pig roast. We all had the Hawaii 5-0 get up on with Foster Grants. My friend had a daughter,

I remember after the beautiful wedding, me and my wife sat with her. I remember talking to her. She said, "Oh, what a beautiful wedding. I got to see my brother get married. I can't wait until I'm married." I thought she was doing so well.

About six months after that wedding, My friend called me and said, "I need your services again." Services for what? "My daughter. She has passed away. I want you to officiate the service." I was floored. Her daughter grew up with my girls. Of course, I was going to do the funeral. At the same time, I get a call from another friend of the family's. They said, "My dad has passed, and I can't get anybody to do the funeral. Could you just say something nice about him?" Here was the catch about that request: One funeral was in Delta, Ohio, at the Memorial Hall. The other funeral was in the next town over in Wauseon, Ohio, at the funeral home. The only time we could schedule the funerals was an hour apart. It was going to be a challenge, but I agreed to do both funerals. I wrote both sermons. One funeral was at 11 in the morning and finished at noon. I then drove to my friends dad's funeral. The funeral director there said, "Man, you're the Superman of pastors." I feel compelled that all people need to be put to rest with some kind of dignity. When I conduct funerals, I see it as an opportunity to preach to the living and help them heal. I tell the mourners that the deceased's lot is sealed, but to those of us living, can we just hug each other? Take a moment and greet each other.

We shouldn't just get together when tragedy strikes. Then I speak about the good qualities of that person who has passed on.

The next funeral after that was for a young lady. I remembered her as a girl running in and out of the house with my stepdaughter Destiny. They sent her body down to Toledo for the autopsy because we were in the rural areas. Destiny called, and she took over planning everything; I called her the event director. She came down from Port Huron, Michigan, to bury her friend. I typed up a fundraising flier. When Destiny came to town, we held a fundraiser, I was out there to pray over the ceremony. By noon, we had raised a lot of money for the funeral. I've never been so proud of the community. They pulled together, brought that girl home, and she had the dignified funeral service she deserved. I did her funeral, and there wasn't a dry eye in the house. "God called me from out of darkness to where I am." My unique background allows me to call up the strength to do what I have to do. My objective is all about the family of the deceased.

My cousin, Carmelita, spent her whole life begging and pleading with me to get off the streets. Most of my girl cousins were older than me and watched me come home from the hospital when I was a baby. Whenever they would see me out there driving the cars and wearing the jewelry, those cousins would cry. My other cousin, Linda Thomas, was a court official and worked with people who tried to bond out. She would see me in shackles trying to bond out or on my way to court, and she would just bawl and say, "Oh my God, will you just stop!" But they still hugged me and were determined to save my life. They couldn't fathom I became a pistol-toting gangster with two other guys flanking me, and I never hid it. Even many attempts on my life and getting shot at and being left for dead in 1986 didn't stop me. I got half of my arm shot off by a .357 magnum. A guy I grew up with and me were fighting over a disagreement over drug turf. I was a one-armed gangster until I regained mobility of that injured arm.

Life in Toledo had toughened me up for anything. We went from occasional selling of nickel and dime bags of weed to making more money than we had ever seen circulating in the city in our life. There were 15- and 16-year-olds driving Mercedes. They could wreck and tear those up and just buy another one. Guys just getting all the gold teeth they wanted. I walked into stores and bought 15 or 20 pairs of Jordans and Polo shirts for my crew—and the guy over there who looked like he wished had one, I'd buy him one, too. That was the mindset of people in the city: Reward was worth the risk to them. They were willing to shoot it out with whoever. You wouldn't open a trap house if it couldn't make at least $2,000 a day. I was a name brand, the Monty Hall of the drug gangs. It was Let's Make a Deal all day long. I never let anyone get away with their money. I would sell them anything, from a key of cocaine to a $14 piece of cocaine . . . because that's $14 I didn't have before. I would accommodate anybody.

After I had gotten out of jail one time, I knew it would take a while for me to get back on my feet on the streets. My enemies had known I had gotten out of jail, knew I wasn't in full force, and that I'd be vulnerable. I was slithering around town trying to get things going, always aware my rivals would kill me before I could rise back to power, or they would have tricked me to thinking they were on my side. I knew I had to fly under the radar until I was strong enough to show myself. During this time, I saw a guy with dirty clothes on always fixing cars. This guy comes to me one day and says, "Hey,." I cut him off and said, "Hey, that's OK, I don't need any car work done." He said, "I'm not selling car work, man. Look under that tire." Under that tire was half a key of cocaine. He said, "All of this is me. I like to fix cars for a hobby. If you don't come back here, you only beat yourself. If you come back, there's plenty more. I've been watching you, and I know you're a professional. You just need a hand up." This man was a multi-millionaire, but he never forgot where he came from. His dad ran gas stations, and he was a mechanic by trade, so that's why he still worked on cars. He had a hunch about me, he trusted me, and he invested in me. I invest in people, too, to this day. A lot of people don't have anybody who believes in them. They might need that one person who says, "You can do that." I have several people in my groups that have their own businesses now and are very successful. When they got sober, they would say things like, "All I do is home repair and drywall." Those are useful skills. I got them to get in business, to get a license, and get advertising. It's not complicated: Whatever you have to do to use your skills and get in business. Quite naturally, my supervisors would cynically ask me, "Why are you telling those people that they can work in this field, and they can do this and they can do that?" My answer was always the same: "Because they can." I said to the naysayers, "Look at me. Look what I'm doing." They would claim that I was different, but I say I'm no different than anybody else. Only thing I never lacked was confidence. I always believed in myself. That was instilled in me from my mom and dad. We were told we could be anything if we put our mind to it and if we were willing to work for it. Even though I knew that lesson, I had not always put it into practice when I was making money on the street. When I would take a plea deal instead of going to trial, the judge would always ask me if I was under the influence of any alcohol or narcotics or did anybody promise me anything. The judge knew doggone well that I struck a deal with the prosecutor and the lawyer under the table. I was instructed to say "no" for the record. I was supposed to forfeit $60,000 and the Benz and the Jag, and I had to make an impact statement to the court and apologize 100 times to my community, even though I wasn't sorry. I bought two years for $60,000, instead of 20. I could make that kind of money just roaming around alone on the street. I had come to a point in my life where I had to put into practice what my parents had taught me.

When I straightened my life out and got back in the ministry, I got promoted to counselor after I earned my CDCA, which meant I could conduct chemical dependency groups. As long as I was working under a therapist or social worker or another counselor, I could conduct groups. When they turned me loose on the groups, it wasn't long before it yielded amazing results. People wanted to be in my groups, and it was because I made things simple. I would always say, "Why are we making this complicated?" These group members' minds have been damaged by alcohol, drugs, and other kinds of abuse, so they need time for their mind to heal. There was no need to force a rigid curriculum on them like they were college students. I broke it down and started simplifying things, like it was done on Sesame Street or Electric Company. For example, on the first day of a dual diagnostic group (a mental health and substance use disorder group), I say, "Let's go around the room and introduce yourself." If someone says, "My name is so-and-so and I'm an addict," I stop them and say, "I'm not concerned about you being an addict. Please just tell me if you're a mother or a daughter or a father or a neighbor, but don't tell me about you being an addict. I want to know who you really are because I'm trying to bring back the remembrance to you of another time. I want to know you played some high school football, or you were the prom queen, and celebrate the old you. Then you can heal and hold your head high again and not walk in shame." My reason for doing this was that if I keep reminding someone of their faults, how can they move on? For example, if I got in a bad accident, I'm not going to go back to that same intersection and keep reliving the same trauma and the same pain. I believe that we need to be mindful when reminding people of their faults; they're more than that. To let them see that, sometimes I would do this assignment. I assign someone who has some artistic ability to go to the board and draw a tombstone. I then have someone who can spell well take over. I tell the group, "We're having a funeral and services today. We got some things that have to go in our life, like selfishness, or sadness, or anger. We're going to fill this tombstone up with all the stuff that's got to go." Then I'll take the tombstone and draw a bridge going across to a blank shield/coat of arms. I ask the group about the things they admire in other people's lives. What would they want for their kids? None of our mothers brought us home and said, "I want my kid to be a little drunk, or I want my kid to be a homeless person. That would be so cool." Sometimes people who are stuck in certain "accepted" treatment approaches come out and say, "Rob, they say you hate the 12 steps." I say, "No, I hate what they've done to the 12 steps." Those guys who founded Alcoholics Anonymous described having an epiphany of some kind that gave them a blueprint. It was a failed business meeting, and it led to AA. They altered the Bible to something like near beer. It's like me saying, "Give me some fake beers, and I'll pretend I'm drinking." For example, the first step in AA talks about your life becoming unmanageable. I say, "Well, who allowed your life to become unmanageable? Who gave the power to alcohol and drugs over you?" My approach is more about now that you're sober, I'm going to teach you how to keep your power and not give it to anybody else. I'm going to educate you to be self-sufficient; I'm not going to teach broken person syndrome. I'm going to teach you to be self-sufficient and go out and find the boldness to live and go after your dreams and goals. I'm talking about something bigger than pity parties because I don't do pity parties. I'm constantly breathing life into my groups.

When we cross over the bridge from the tombstone, I want them to know they're getting rid of their old life. It's going to be a journey. I know. When I did it, I had sunshine and I had rain on the way to getting from the dead life to the new life. As they are on that new journey, I have to let them know what to do in a way that makes sense. Since I had been down that road, I can relate to them. I tell them that we have to be in compliance, take ownership of what we've done, and realize the part we played to get us in this position. I know we live in the USA, the greatest country ever stole. I know it's the American way to commit crime, and I know we've got two political parties that promote deceit and dishonesty. It doesn't make it right. Just because everyone is doing it, it doesn't make it right. I write the word "integrity" on the board and ask the group what that word means to them. What do you do when no one is looking? We have to be the same person and act the same way when someone is watching.

I use visual teaching until the group is ready to go to the next phase. Again, I try to keep it simple because otherwise it gets intimidating. I'm pushing independence and self-reliance. A lot of people respond to that, but I'm also constantly looking to make adjustments and changes. They say Bill Belichick is one of the greatest coaches who ever lived, and Tom Brady is one of the greatest quarterbacks. Why do they say that? It's because they can make in-the-game adjustments. Derrick Rose is the hardest working basketball player. With his injuries, his career was taken from him, so he worked hard to get it back. No one worked harder to get back. He set the tone for the younger guys to give their best. I approach my therapy groups like I'm the Belichick, Brady, and Rose of the counseling world. When I'm in game, the classroom is my arena. I'm going to make the adjustments, so I will reach you. Jerks in the group? Bring them on. Smart alecks in the group? Bring them on. Clowns? I can handle clowns. I can handle the lion. I'm the ringmaster. I'm the guy with the black boots in the center of the circus. That's how I was in the street.

There's a difference between an inmate and convict. An inmate is a guy that comes into prison, follows the rules, and doesn't want any trouble; he just wants to do the time and get out of there. Then there's the convict. A convict can make a weapon out of anything and knows how to work the system. Let's just say I was a convict. I trained the guards in prison. When rookie guards came on the job, I would tell them what to do and what not to do. They all knew me. We pulled time together in Mansfield, in Lima, and in Belmont, near West Virginia. I knew who to stay away from. My test was: If he ain't coming right, he's a convict. I was capable of anything if pushed. If you corner a convict, he's not in there without a way out. He will survive at all costs.

My past as a convict certainly helped me in my new life. One example is from when I was doing a class at Fresh Start. Three wannabe Aryan Brotherhood guys that came from doing some minor prison time were in the group with their little swastikas and their attitudes. Every time I would ask them a question, they would say jerk things like, "I don't like you, but I have to be in this group." They would also try to torment the one Black guy and one Mexican guy who didn't speak English well. They were acting like it was their own fraternity. My patience was wearing thin, so I prayed and said, "God, I'm trying not to smack these punks in the next week." Guess what God does? On Monday, new arrivals showed up in the group. And who shows up? A guy we used to fight with at Mansfield. Unlike the hecklers in the group, Larry had been a real member in the Aryan Brotherhood. He was covered in swastikas and lightning bolts. I had to take a second and pray again by saying, "God, that's not funny."

Larry comes into the room, looked at me, and said, "Don't I know you from somewhere?" I decided to play it safe and said, "Nah, probably not. I got a face like that." Larry gave me another look like he knew me but just couldn't place me. A few days go by in group, and Larry puts up with those three wannabe Aryans asking him about his tattoos. Guys in the Aryan Brotherhood can't have certain tattoos, like skull and crossbones or Irish Celtic ones, unless they had earned them, so Larry's tats impressed those three clowns. On the third day of those jerks talking their usual smack, Larry finally stood up and told them, "I want you punks to shut up." Larry then pointed at me and said, "That man could kill you. I know this man. You don't want to be involved with that. Let me tell you something. I spent 30 years wasting my life being a flunky for the brotherhood. I'm a Christian now, and I'm saved." I silently thanked Jesus for that. Larry went on and said, "I'm saved. And this man"—referring to me again— "has come a long way. I remember when this man would have cut you young punks from ear to ear for saying anything he thought was racist. This man fought every day. I'm so proud of this man. I want you to know I wish I could take all of these tattoos off me. I want to hug that man; he's my brother." Better late than never for Larry remembering who I was! Also, those three wannabe Aryans behaved themselves after that.

Me and Larry stayed in contact for two years after that. He told me about his progress with his kids and his biracial grandchildren that he was healing with. It was just amazing. He turned his life over to God and denounced separatists. Larry walked the walk, no doubt about it. There was an older Black guy who was a big-time drug dealer, and he had a stroke. He was so bitter and mean about what happened to him. Larry, a guy who had stabbed Blacks and Mexicans for being another race, stepped up and took care of that man like he was his own father. He cleaned up his drool, he carried him around, he wheeled him around. Even though that old Black drug dealer screamed and yelled at Larry, Larry told him, "I'm going to take care of you. I don't care how mad you get at me. You can't take care of yourself, so I'm going to do it." What an act of love. I know God has the ability to change people's heart. You don't always have to be what you were.

Feeling good. Ready to watch my Great niece graduate from Kentucky State University.

In the office getting some inspiration.

Feeling fresh.

9

INFLUENCERS

In the Bible, God created Adam and gave Adam some authority and dominion. It's like that scene with Eddie Murphy in the movie Trading Places. When Eddie starts stealing cigars from those old white guys, they tell Eddie, "You're only stealing from yourself." One of my biggest and earliest inspirations came from when I watched that TV show called Ironside when I was a kid. That detective had lost his legs, but it didn't stop him from being a cop. If Ironside could do stuff and succeed, what's my excuse?

Selena and I got married on a Wednesday night, August 25th, 2010, at Delta Assembly of God, the same church where I experienced my revelation. When I turned my life over to God, I saw Selena in a different light and wanted her to be my wife and my lifelong helpmate. So, we called Pastor Randy Trowbridge up and ask him to marry us. Pastor Randy, he said he would only perform the ceremony after counseling us. Pastor Randy had known Selena all her life, and after counseling me, he was concerned about her choice in a husband. Pastor Randy was from Wisconsin and was a Badger and Packer fan. He was also so concerned about me that he went to my in-laws-to-be and asked, "How long has Selena known this guy?" Pastor Randy wasn't concerned that I was Black. This area I lived in wasn't racist, but there just was never many Black people living there. It was kind of like that movie Guess Who's Coming to Dinner with Sidney Portier.

My stepmom is Marilyn Lomas. My dad had been married to her for 25 years before he passed. Marilyn had stuck with me through all of my incarcerations. She believed in me and loved me so much that her nickname for me was "The Good Son." People wondered why she called me that when most people saw me as the spawn of Satan! She said she would speak that nickname over me until I changed and, finally, I did. Before Pastor Randy married us, my stepmom put the flower in Selena's hair. Our wedding was one of the few times everybody in the Lomas family was together. It was a perfect wedding in a country church. Folks in Delta sure knew how to throw a shindig. After we were married, we went before the church to praise God together, then we had the festivities.

Shortly after the wedding, I went to Pastor Randy, and he was the one who gave me advice before I did my first funeral service in Toledo. He told me, "Never assume you know how somebody feels. Always stay away from that." Pastor Randy saw that I was a fixer by nature, and he was a huge help to me during my first services. He is a very humble and soft-spoken guy. He had a huge influence on me and my ministry. God sent Pastor Randy to me, no doubt. It was similar to the Bible story of Saul on the road to Damascus. I didn't know what I was going to do once I couldn't hustle anymore. I just had no stomach for it anymore after God called on me. I never had a scheme again, and never drank again.

My father-in-law, Danny Johnson, is a layman preacher, and my wife's uncle Herb is a pastor. Danny and Herb are from Midford, Ohio, which is down by the West Virginia/Ohio border. Both men served in Vietnam. While everybody else was getting drafted, they stepped up and enlisted. They said they knew they were hillbillies, and they at least knew where they were going. When Danny and Herb were on leave together in Germany, they noticed two twins: Emma and Mary. Mary is my mother-in-law. Danny and Herb married Mary and Emma and brought them back to their small town. Coincidentally, my birthday is the same as Emma and Mary's: November 21st. Emma and Mary say it's worse enough they have to share a birthday with each other, now they have a nephew and a son-in-law that hogs the day up, too. All of them have been active in community ministry for years. Even though Danny and Herb are both preachers, they are as different as day and night as far as they approach the ministry. Danny writes spiritual poetry and is very a mellow guy. Herb, on the other hand, is an old school "hell and brimstone" type, and he will tell you the truth whether you're ready for it or not. He's not going to tickle your ears. I learned something from both of them, and they have been major influences on me.

From my father-in-law, Danny, I learned what it meant, and what it consisted of, to be a person of action, to be a spiritual leader of the family, and to sacrifice to God. Danny is all about faith. He has to have blind faith if he's a Detroit Lions fan! I see him at the store, and he's got a smile on his face with his Lions jacket on, and I tease him by saying, "I'm glad you're living your best life now that you turned all these dysfunctional kids over to me!" From Uncle Herb , I learned to stand on the promises of God even when people think you're crazy for doing so. I learned boldness in Christ from him. It's all about accountability, not handouts. It's about what you can do for God and your community. Herb is as old school as they get.

Herb kind of reminds me of my dad, may he rest in peace, who was extremely strict on us growing up. He wanted us to know life was not always fair, and he wanted us to be without excuses in life. As long as I can remember, one of the things my dad would always say to us since we were kids was, "Weak men strive on sympathy. You'll get none. There's nothing wrong with you. Get up and keep moving." He wouldn't host any pity parties. He would say to my mom about my brothers and me, "I'm raising men, not boys." He would say to me when I was rolling in money, "Rob, you can't do nothing without God. What you're doing, it ain't gonna last. I don't care how much you make or steal, you're not gonna find peace with it." I didn't want to hear that, but it turned out to be so true.

Another thing my dad did that has stayed with me happened whenever I was thrown in jail. I would call him so I could get some help, so he could sign the bond to bail me out. He would do it, but he would want me to suffer for a while. I would try to calm him down from reacting to my behavior and say on our call, "Dad, I heard a speaker, and someone you know from the church came and I quoted some scripture." My dad would get quiet, and then he would say, "I'm not interested in you quoting scripture. The devil knows scripture. He's been to heaven and I ain't. He was there when it was getting written. I ain't impressed. I want to know what you're living; I don't want to know what you're talking about." I would get so mad at him. Then he'd say, "Look, I'm not trying to be funny, but I have some guests here and we're cooking out and you could be here too if you follow rules and regulations in society. Other than that, we got things to do. Bye." Other times he would tell me, "If you were a slow learner or had special needs or something like that, I would accept this behavior from you. But you're choosing to live like the scum of the earth. I can't accept this from an intelligent person. If you could figure out how to run a whole dope racket or gambling organization, you could figure out how to get a real job or open a business." He was right. I find myself more like my father now.

From my mother, Frances Lomas, I was also made aware that God was there for me if I was willing to accept Him. She made sure I had a healthy Christian upbringing and that I knew the value of family and community. If I had not had that type of upbringing, I believe it would have been far more difficult for me to get where I'm am.

My mom and dad were Southern Baptists in the late 1960s and early 1970s. Our family did everything with the church. We came there early in the morning for Sunday school and might not leave there until the evening. The church would cook food for everybody. One of the early experiences I had was with Reverend James Oliphant. He was a big giant man, and he reminded me of the football player Rosy Grier. Reverend Oliphant would preach until he was sweating his suit and until he didn't have a voice anymore. He was committed to delivering the word. He was like a cross between James Brown and Little Richard. Like James Brown singing "Please." Nobody could beg like James Brown or Otis Redding. Reverend Oliphant had a huge influence on me because he would go down the aisles and would want nothing more than to reach individuals. I teach like that. When I teach in group, I'm hands on and challenge each individual right where they're at. I will always be straightforward with you. As I say and believe, it's always about accountability. I make sure my clients know that if they are accountable for their action, I am available to them 24/7.

My personality can intimidate other people in the ministry. I'm confident but not flashy. I'm confident in God more so than in my abilities. I can't fix everybody, but God can. I come into helping each person expecting something positive to happen. I'm coming in with my sleeves rolled up when I'm working with somebody. I expect total recovery, and I'm promoting total recovery and total balance. That attitude is a good influence on people and breeds long term success.

On our way to Tennessee to officiate my daughter's wedding.

10

FAMILY

I write about my family in more detail in the first volume of my life, but I'd like to honor them here again and also add a more recent story about a new family member.

My mother, Frances, was the fourth of five girls born to Bowling and Naomi Garrett. The Garrett family was from Clarksville, Tennessee, and migrated to Sylvania, Ohio. Life for my mother's family in Sylvania, Ohio, in the 1950s was not much better than back in the Jim Crow South. I once looked at my mother and my aunt's high school yearbook, and what I saw shocked and haunted me. My mother and aunts had to take their picture separate from their Caucasian classmates. To add insult to injury, the only thing written identifying their pictures was the caption that simply read, "The Garnett girls." My mother and her sisters always prided themselves on using proper grammar and having a good educational foundation. My mother instilled in us that we could do anything we put our mind to, and if you can conceive it, you can achieve it. My father, Edmond, was also known to his friends as Jack. The original spelling of our name is "Lomax." Once my ancestor was freed from slavery, he dropped the "x" and added the "s," officially making it "Lomas." So, we also have some Lomax relatives out there. My dad was born to Lucille and Bo Jack Lomas in Denham Springs, Louisiana. He had siblings named Irma, Emma, Ali, and Robert. However, my dad would discover later in life that he had other siblings from after his parents had broke up, and those siblings had the last name of Morris. Like many other Blacks from the deep South who were trying to escape the horrors of the Ku Klux Klan and Jim Crow laws, my dad migrated north and arrived in Holland, Ohio, sometime in the 1950s. I found it interesting that my dad did not permit us to identify anyone by size or color because he said he lived through that in the racist South, and he wanted us to be better than his oppressor. My brother, Larry, made that mistake once when he called the next-door neighbor kid "Red" because of the color of his hair. Needless to say, my dad made sure Larry never made that mistake again. My dad met my mother and they courted briefly, fell in love, and got married.

My oldest brother, Edmond, is named, of course, after my father, and he was called "Jacky" so there would be no confusion when my mother called for my dad whose nickname was Jack. Jacky excelled in running track and earned a scholarship to Jackson Community College. He lives in Detroit, Michigan, and my love for sport came from him. Delano is my second oldest brother, and we call him "Deeney" for short. Deeney loved all kinds of music. He always read a lot, dreamed about seeing the world, and that's exactly what he did. He left home right after high school, joined the Navy, and made a career out of it. He retired and lives in New Orleans, Louisiana. Deeney exposed me to other cultures and music. I can still remember the first time he allowed me to listen to his headset and introduced me to Jimi Hendrix's Electric Ladyland, Carole King's Tapestry, and Chicago's V.

My third oldest brother is Erwin, but we call him Jerome. Jerome was also good in sports. He was a Golden Glove champ and also excelled in track and field. I am grateful to Jerome because he was the one who taught me how to survive and how to think in the streets. I remember him telling me often, "Rob, always stay away from cliques, gangs, and organizations . . . unless it's your own."

My sister, Pamela, or Pam as we called her, was the only girl in the family. She was also very talented; she could sing, and she also excelled in track. I owe a lot to Pam because she taught me how to cook and sew. Tragically, she died along with my mother and two younger half-brothers in a house fire. I love Pam and miss her so much.

My brother, Larry, is the sibling closest in age to me, and we did everything together growing up. He always protected me and made sure I stayed out of trouble—for a while at least! He also helped me understand the Bible in a way that relates to our everyday life. We still talk daily about all topics.

My youngest stepdaughter Destiny is super gifted and keeps us on our toes. She has a heart for helping people. She motivates me to be better. I look forward to watching her grow in her gifts as she is now my operations Manager. My other stepdaughter, Marissa, is a girly girl, who calls me Dad. She has always embraced me as a father. I love to play guitar while she sings. Finally, there is Jessica, who had our first grandchild. She is a free spirit. I always enjoy having conversations with her about current events. All three of these girls have been a gift from God, I will always treasure. They have been there to see my conversion up close and have always been supportive, even with our disagreements. The funny thing is, my kids go to Selena when they want something, and my stepdaughters come to me when they want something. Rashawnda has always been a Daddy's girl. The sun sets and rises around me. She has always worked hard and has been strong, fearless, and independent. Little Rob is my junior. He's thoughtful and strong and a lot like me. He's creative and blessed with an entrepreneurial spirit. I talk to Rob every morning. My next youngest son, Elijah, was raised on the West Coast, and he inherited my exceptional athletic ability. I've always excelled in any kind of sport, be it basketball, football, track, darts, and even marbles. Elijah also inherited my vision and the discipline to follow through on things. Finally, Javontay, or J.J. as we are calling him, moved in with me, Selena, and Destiny when he was 13 years old. We took him to church, and he was involved with all the programs. Selena loves him as if he was her own. He has a good heart and always roots for the underdog.

I have another daughter named Destiny who was born 16 years ago in December. When Destiny was born, I was still actively involved in the drug business. Destiny was placed with Brenda and Barry Stotler. Meanwhile, Destiny's mom and I tried to get our act together, but unfortunately, we failed. I remember the very last visit I had with baby Destiny. Brenda, Barry, and Destiny's mother had made up their mind that if anything happened that would keep us from regaining custody of Destiny, then Brenda and Barry would adopt Destiny. It was the best decision, especially because I went off to serve my last stint in prison after that. Often over the years, Brenda would randomly email me pictures of Destiny growing up, playing the violin and dancing, and updates about what she was doing. I agreed I would not intrude on her upbringing, and when it was her time to ask about me, so be it. And Lord behold, it happened. When Destiny was a sophomore in high school, she told Brenda and Barry, "I think it's time to find out where I come from." We agreed to have dinner in 2022. We met halfway from Toledo, where Destiny was, and Wauseon, where I was. We met in the middle (coincidentally, in Holland, Ohio, where I was born), at a small Mideastern/Mediterranean restaurant called Grape Leaf. Everything in that place looked like you were really in the Middle East. I don't remember why I chose that place, but something told me to pick it. It turned out Destiny's adoptive parents were Christians. Before we sat down, we all prayed. I said, "I want to thank you guys because you've done an amazing job. This was clearly the best option for Destiny." There wasn't a dry eye at the table. I'm Creole descendant from Louisiana and Destiny's biological mother was full German. Destiny said she was aware of her German side, but she didn't know much about my side. I let her know where her grandparents were from on my side. Barry and I had football in common, even though he was a Lions fan, and I was a Browns fan. We both had our years of torment with rooting for losing teams. We were also both Ohio State Buckeye fans. They are amazing parents.. I said to her, "I don't know why God is telling me to tell you this, but I want to leave you with something of substance whether you ever allow me to talk to you again or not." I said, "Listen to me well. Never lower or compromise your morals or Christian values that your parents instilled in you. You are a young Christian lady, and you don't have to lower your standards for anyone ever!" Brenda and Barry seemed happy I was who I was. Everybody was proud of the transformation I made. They watched me and followed me. They thought it was amazing. They agreed they would come to my church and that we would get together once a month to do something. From that one meeting, I could tell

Destiny had my eyes, and she's a very whimsical and clever girl. How fitting for my life to come full circle and meet for the very first time my last biological child right down the street where I was born. It was another divine occurrence in my life.

I'm seated on the left. In the middle is my sister Pam and to the far right, my brother Larry. Summer of 1972, Toledo.

My amazing, beautiful wife, Mrs. Selena Lomas. I would not have gotten here without her.

My Mom and I on my wedding Day!

My son, Jayvontay and I at my daughter's wedding in 2020.

My son Elijah and I.

My daughter, Destiny.

My girls Jessica, Marrisa, and Destiny in 2022.

Myself, Bother's Jerome and Pete at Shamar's wedding.

My Mother Francis Lomas

Me and little Rob on his Birthday.

Me and my daughter Rashawnda.

My lovely wife and I at home in Wauseon Ohio

11

BENEDICTION

Like my dad before me, I never met a stranger. My dad could talk to everybody. I get referrals from former Klan members and Aryan Brotherhood. When guys like that first meet me, they're thinking, Why would the judge refer me to you? You're Black. When we start talking, it doesn't take long for them to realize that I'm their guy. Why? Because I've lived with white supremacists and militant Muslims in institutions. Prison is a breeding ground for religious fanatics and people looking for something. I reach people. I get a lot of unlikely pairings in this community I work in. I'm where God sent me.

Because prison is a breeding ground for religious nuts, that's another reason I am open to all spiritual truths. Some people can't handle the truth. One day in a maximum-security prison in Toledo, inmates were acting crazy, stabbing each other, beating on each other, and looking at each other like they wanted to kill each other. Chris Pierce, who I worked with at Ridge Project, left them envelopes and pens and tablets. He said, "I'm sick to my stomach how you guys are assaulting each other and disrespecting each other as human beings. What I want you all to do is write your last will and testament right now because you're not always going to be the person who comes out on top in these situations in this prison. Just because you live in prison doesn't mean you have to act like savages and animals. If you got anybody out there, write what you want to write now because this isn't going to end good. Raise your hand. Who in here doesn't want to be loved? If you want to be loved, are you putting love in the world? Are you giving love?" There wasn't a dry eye in the place.

Guys on death row plead for mercy, but they never showed any mercy before that. I expound on that when I counsel. I treat people the way I like to be treated. I will be consistent and be the same guy every time. That's just who I am. From those correctional institutions, I learned stuff. I used to be mad and depressed, and I would have rocks in my jaw. Then one day I stumbled across some books in the library: Thomas J. Stanley's Millionaire Next Door and In the Mind of a Millionaire. He interviewed self-made millionaires in the state of Oklahoma. I had no idea Oklahoma has more millionaires than any part of the country. Stanley asked these people what they did to become rich. These people said they were told at a young age they couldn't do certain things. They felt defeated as youngsters, so they used that as motivation, and it drove them. They had creative intelligence. They played their own game and not other people's games. Their attitude was, "You ain't going to beat me at being me." It helped me put a perspective on my strengths and maximize my weaknesses.

I know from experience that people who are broken never reach their full potential or tap into it. Here's a diagnosis that gets thrown around a lot. People will say, "My doctor says I'm bipolar. Sometimes I'm down or up. If I'm cycling in a depressive cycle, it could last for weeks or a month. If I'm in the mania state, I could be running around doing crazy stuff that don't make sense." That's true bipolar. There can be the misinterpretation of something that mimics borderline personality disorder. BPD can cycle throughout the day. Bipolar doesn't cycle like that. Even though I'm not a doctor, I can always give a diagnosis to something. It's like, I used to own a mechanic's shop for 2 years with two lifts. My manager would say, "When someone comes through here, there's always something wrong with the car. We can always find something to check. Never tell them there's nothing wrong with the car. How are we going to stay in business?"

Life throws us curve balls and spit balls. Are we going to go down swinging or go down standing still? A lot of times it's how we respond to the troubles in life that makes a difference. I tell my clients it's human nature to have a tendency to "awfulize" things. If I sit around and look for everything that is wrong, I can find it. I go around the house some days and notice what's falling apart. After a while I work myself into such a frenzy that my wife has to stop me and say, "Stop, honey!" In chaos, we have to get order. One of the things I learned about being in institutions and in red light districts and the city is I billed myself as the King of Chaos.

All the detectives in town knew me by name. I knew their shifts. Regular police had set shifts. Those in the drug task force came on at about 3 a.m., when the bars closed. I wasn't worried about regular cops; they weren't in my league. I could outthink them because they were amateurs on my turf. I had to worry about the guys in the task force. When they get you, it was a celebration. I would come into the 7-11 and they would ask me, "Hey, Rob, busy night?" I would say, "Nah, it was kind of slow actually." We all grew up together. We all played sports together as kids. They became cops, and we became a hustler. A lot of times we all knew each other. We would even be respectful. Danny Navarro was head of the gang task force. There was also Keith "Killer" Miller, who had played college football and then became a cop. He was involved in a few incidents were people lost their lives. Danny and Killer and Melvin Woods were cops who came from the city and were athletes. They would come to me and say, "Rob, cousin, your name is ringing. I can't keep 'em off you. You gotta stop doing what you're doing." They would always tell me when it was going to go bad. They would say, "You need to close your operation down. It's not you, but those guys working for you. There's violence going on, too much shooting. You gotta tone it down." Back then, the crack epidemic mostly took place in the inner city or in red light districts. When the bodies start piling up and killers were being imported from other places, all bets were off and the cops would not look the other way. We were called Holy Toledo for a reason. I never worried about regular police in cruisers. They knew they were dealing with a different league of hustler when it came to me. When they saw our cars, they knew they would have to literally tear it all apart because we had every kind of secret compartment, every kind of fake tennis ball can or battery filled with drugs.

All those detectives liked me and respected me. My reputation was known for being the best bad guy you ever met. Once I came to power, I felt there was no need for me to be cruel. I treated my employees with respect, and I didn't keep them hostage. I looked at how McDonald's and Wendy's operated, and based on those models, I started to franchise my brand, the Rob Lomas brand. I would give other people the formula how I became successful. When a guy showed me he had potential, I would show him how to start his own crew and their own house. You have to have a guy who focuses on security and who watches the house, like a bouncer at a club, and a guy who is good with figures. In those days, we picked upstairs places with one way in, and we would fortify the doors. We made sure it took time when someone had to raid the house. I noticed when I worked at

Wendy's and Fuddruckers, every time when they got to a certain amount of cash, it was moved out of the place so they wouldn't lose money or product. That's how I learned how to run my private enterprise, by mimicking the best.

I consider myself an end-of-the-line therapist and an end-of-the-line preacher. I'm all about accountability. Community Accountability = the Cure. We are all responsible. I'm promoting the steps to get in balance. We have to get the individual in balance before doing anything else. It's similar to a chiropractor who tries to align our back. Our life has to be lined up right. Don't be so busy with life that you forget to live. Live while you're chasing things. Live and feel stuff. Don't pass on going for a walk. Don't wait until you can't walk to wish you could have gone for a walk. Enjoy nature. See all you can see. I was in the Dollar Store the other day, and a lady asked me, "Don't you wish you could be young again?" I said, "Nah, I'm all right." She said, "What do you mean?" There happened to be some young people behind me and I said, I done lived my life and three other peoples' lives. I want to sit down and do nothing!"

A lot of people in the area where I moved to were in denial that people had addiction issues and mental health issues. For example, I did a presentation for some Mennonite ministers about free services. I told them, "I'd like to come to your community and offer my skills." One of the elders said, "It's a nice thing you're doing, young man, but I don't think we have any people like that here." I laughed so hard later on because he was serious. Fast forward, I bet they found out they had plenty of people with problems. The attitude was, "If it doesn't affect me why should I be concerned?" I want to empower people with the knowledge to not only get a meal but be able to fish for themselves. Every one of us has something we can do. There were some guys here that had been the doormen at an old building downtown since 1962. They did their job faithfully and took pride in it. They were honored for their years of hard work. The community got together and honored people who take pride in their work and jobs. We need stories like that, especially when the news is so horrible every time we turn it on.

People ask me what are my degrees in? I say, "I have one degree. I got a degree in what not to do. Only by the grace of God am I'm talking to you." Every time I got thrown back in prison they would say to me, "What are you doing, life on the installment plan? You must not like it in the free world because you keep coming back to us!" Today, I am blessed to run a private practice called RKL Behavioral Health. I am a behavior expert, and I help people change. I'm a licensed chemical dependency counselor. I do motivational speaking and community outreach. I am executive director and founder of Jesus 911 Community Ministries. I am so far removed from my former life. God has blessed me with a new life and a new understanding of what born again means. I feel like I can just live free without the burden of my past. Even though my past is still there, it's no longer a ball and chain that I'm dragging around. I'm looking at the degrees and awards on this wall in my home office, and it's unreal to me. Any time anybody sees me from my past, it's just, like, bizarre. How could this happen? But it's by divine appointment. I just answered the call and was obedient.

Vacation in Pigeon Forge, Tennessee.

Spending time in Tennessee.

My wife in 2014.

StoryTerrace

CPSIA information can be obtained
at www.ICGtesting.com
Printed in the USA
BVHW021357250822
645510BV00021B/450